NathanKapnicky a.k.a. Nate Kap, has enjoyed drawing the characteristics of the face since he was 3 years old. He began caricatures professionally in 2006 and has grown an extreme passion for finding the uniqueness of his subjects. 4 years in the making, he now brings you his vision from the world of the **BEASTED**.

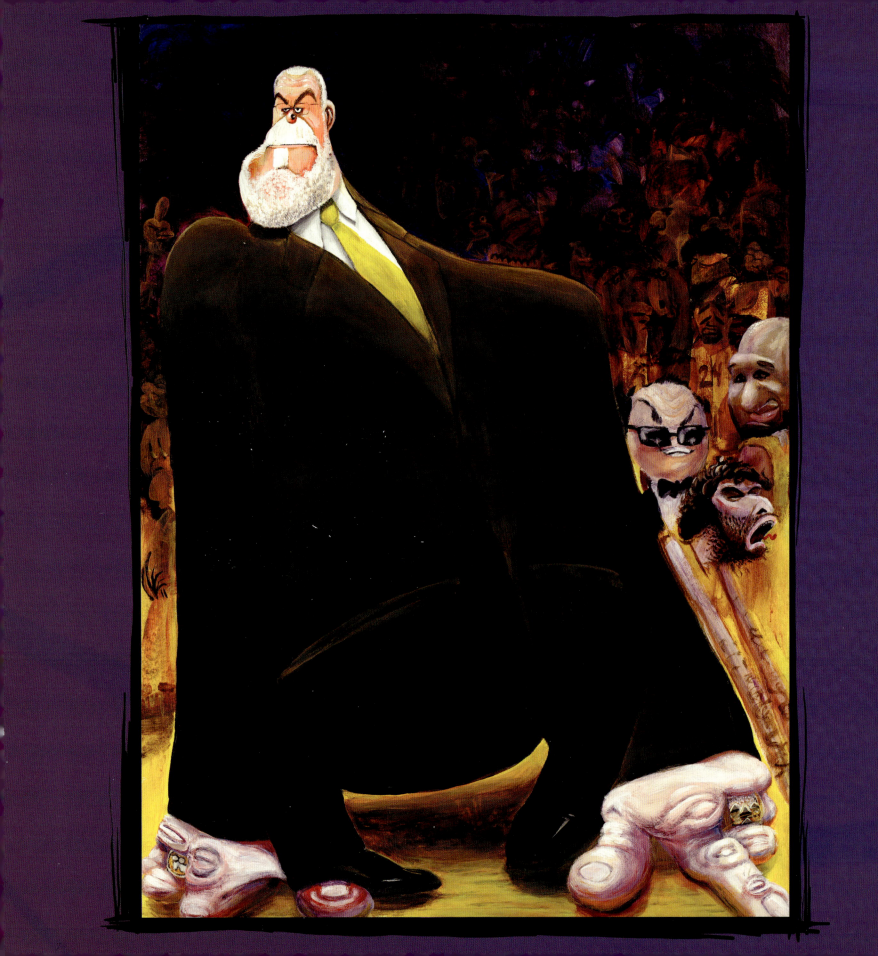

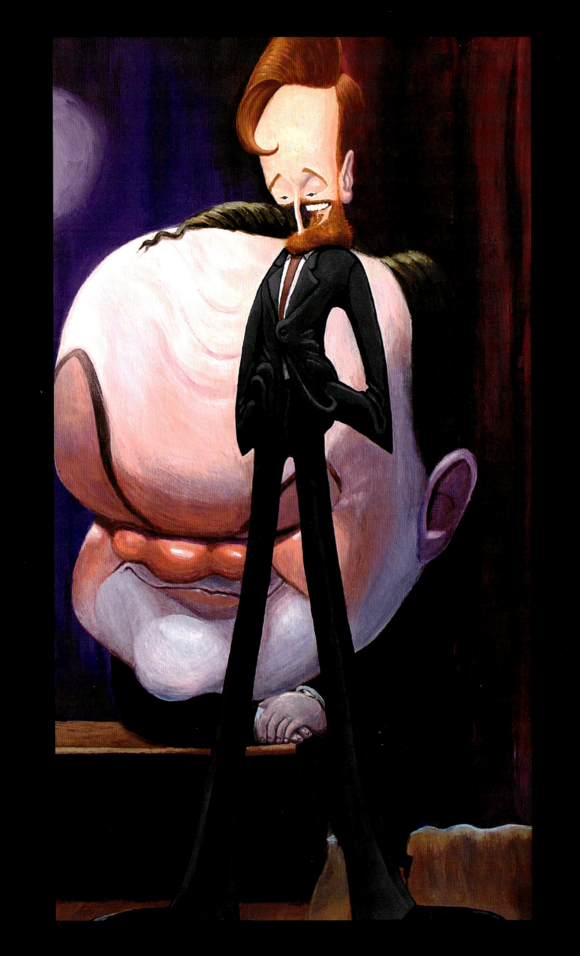

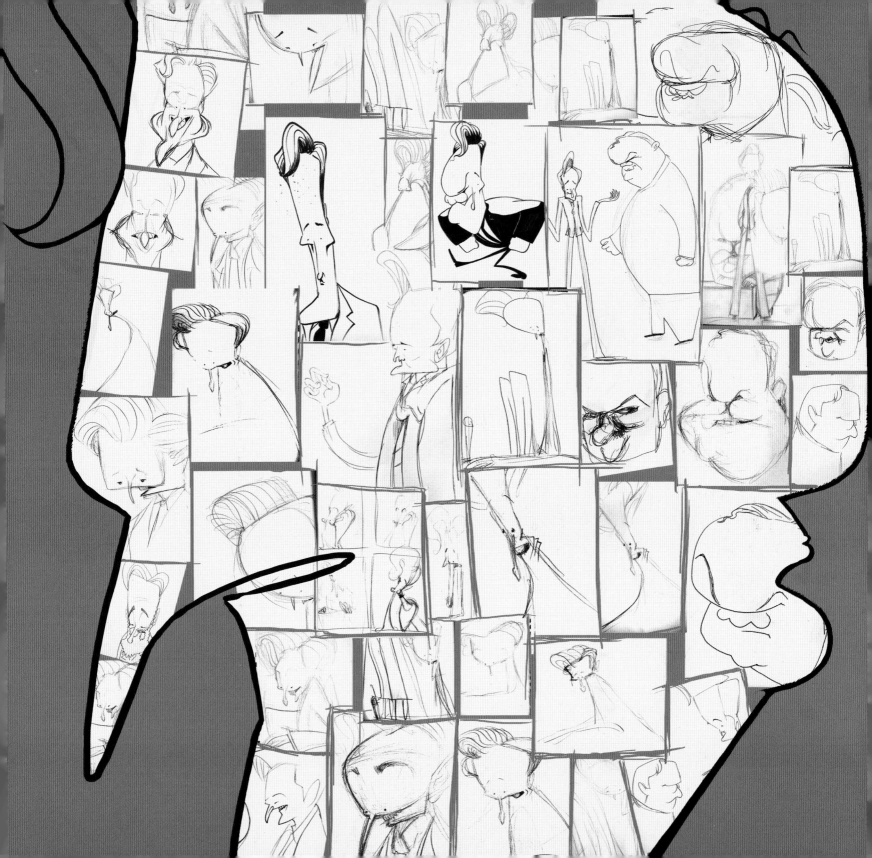

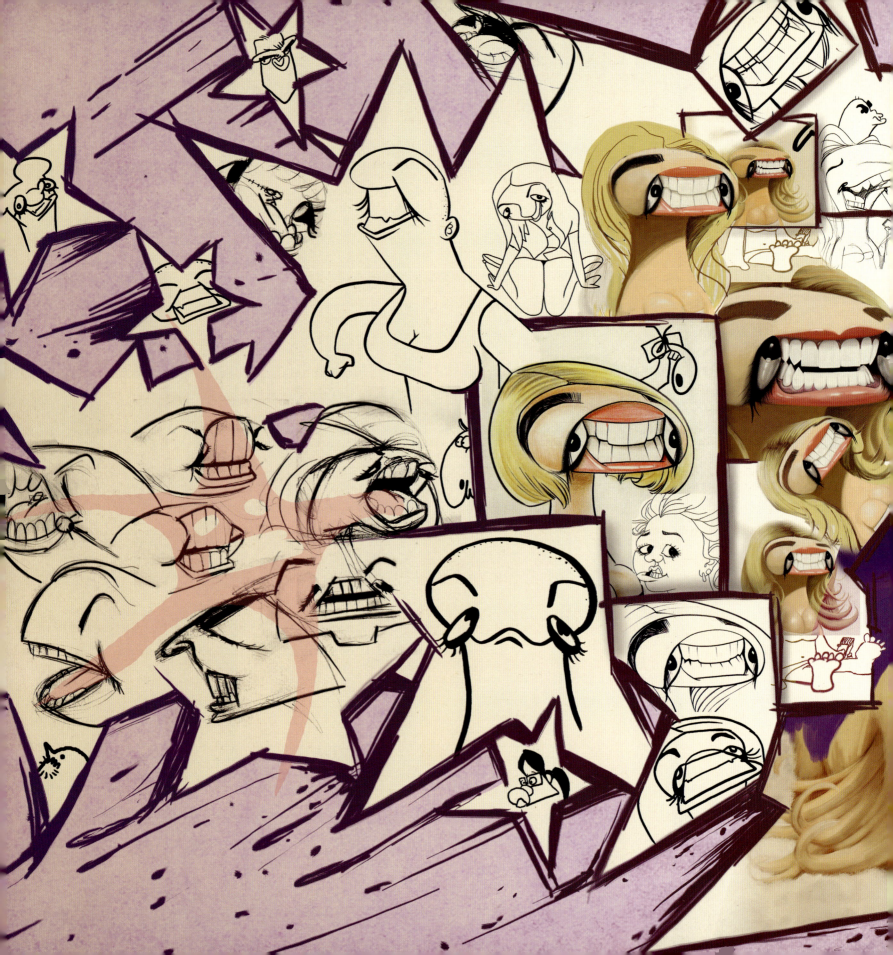

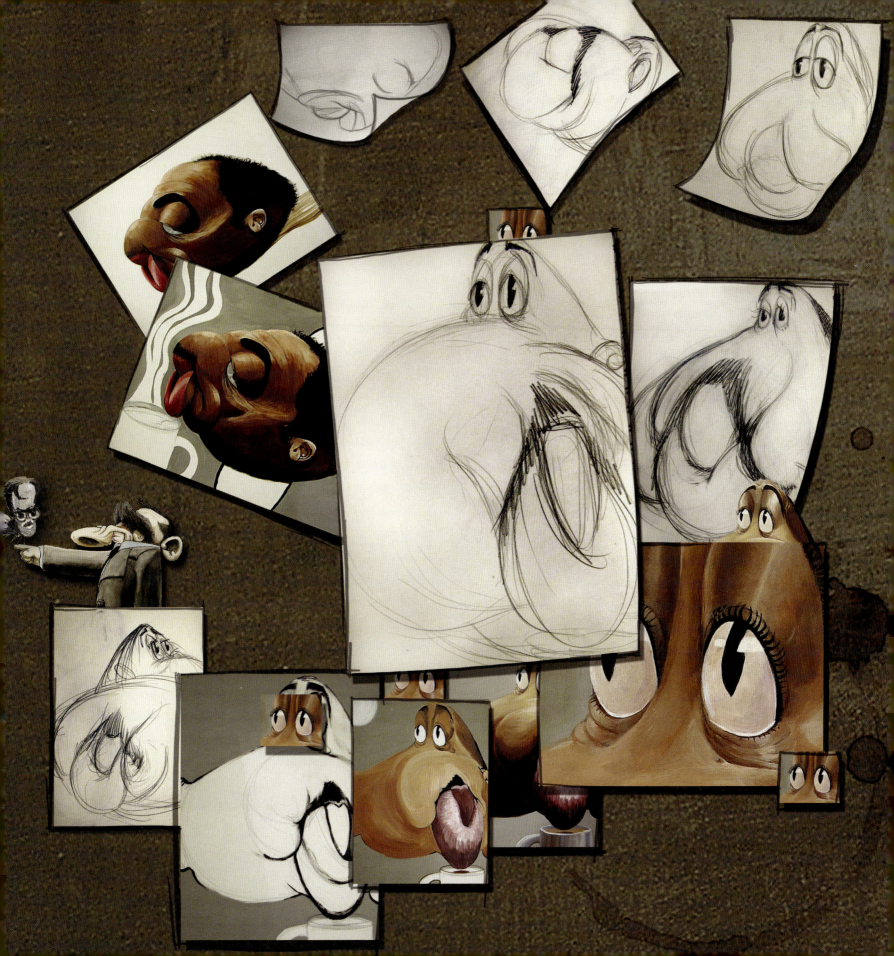

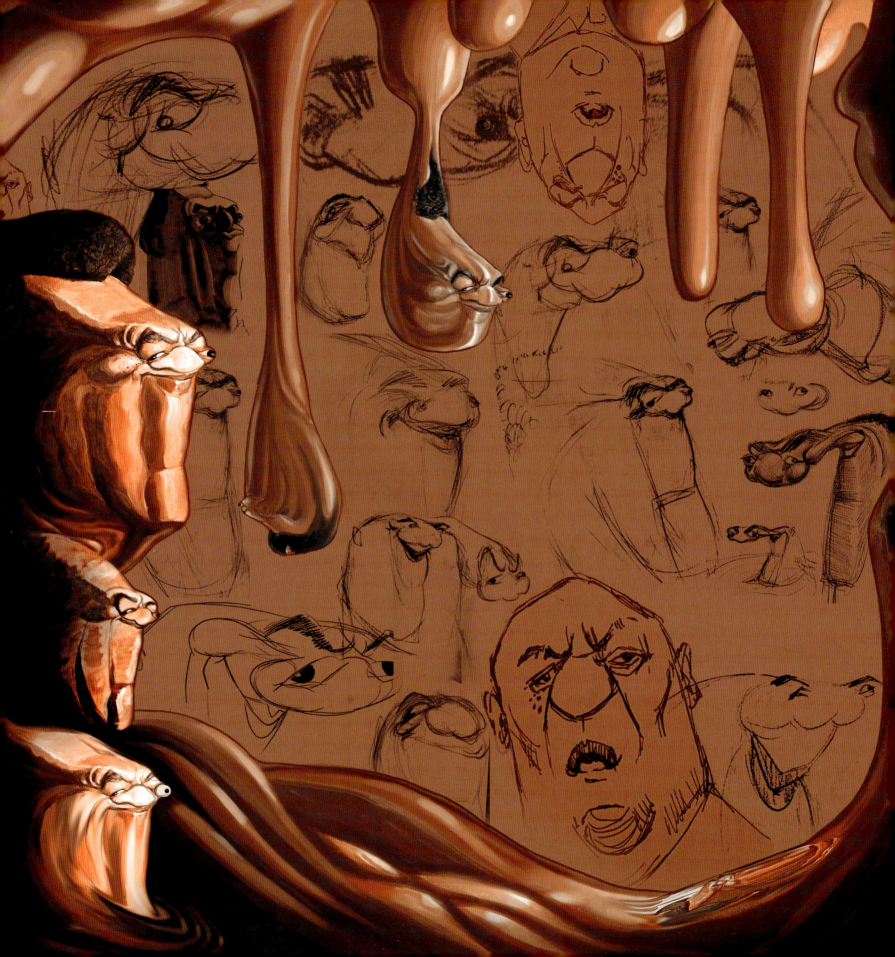

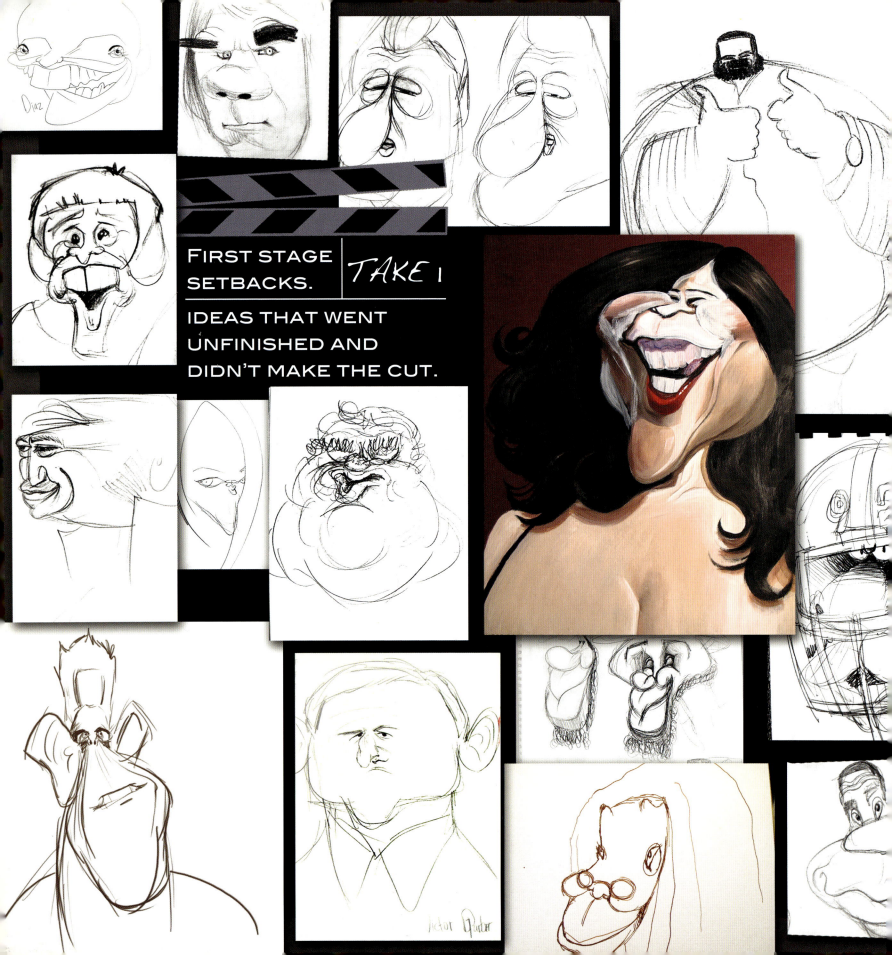

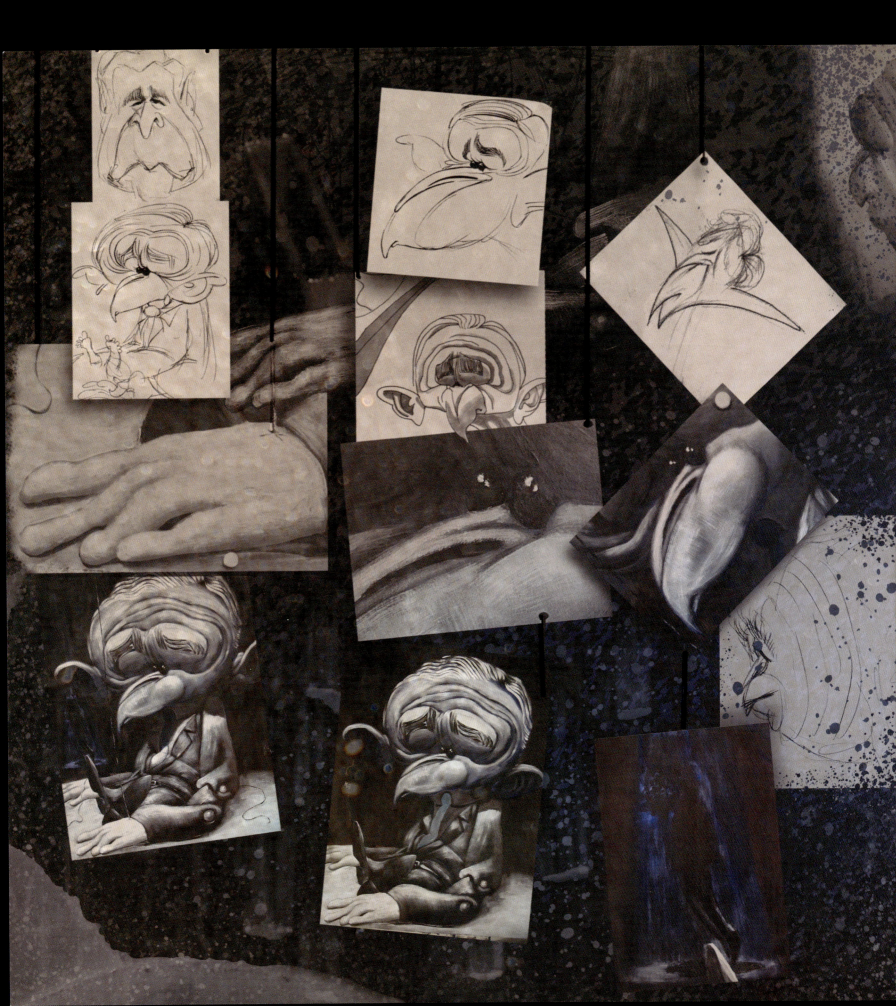

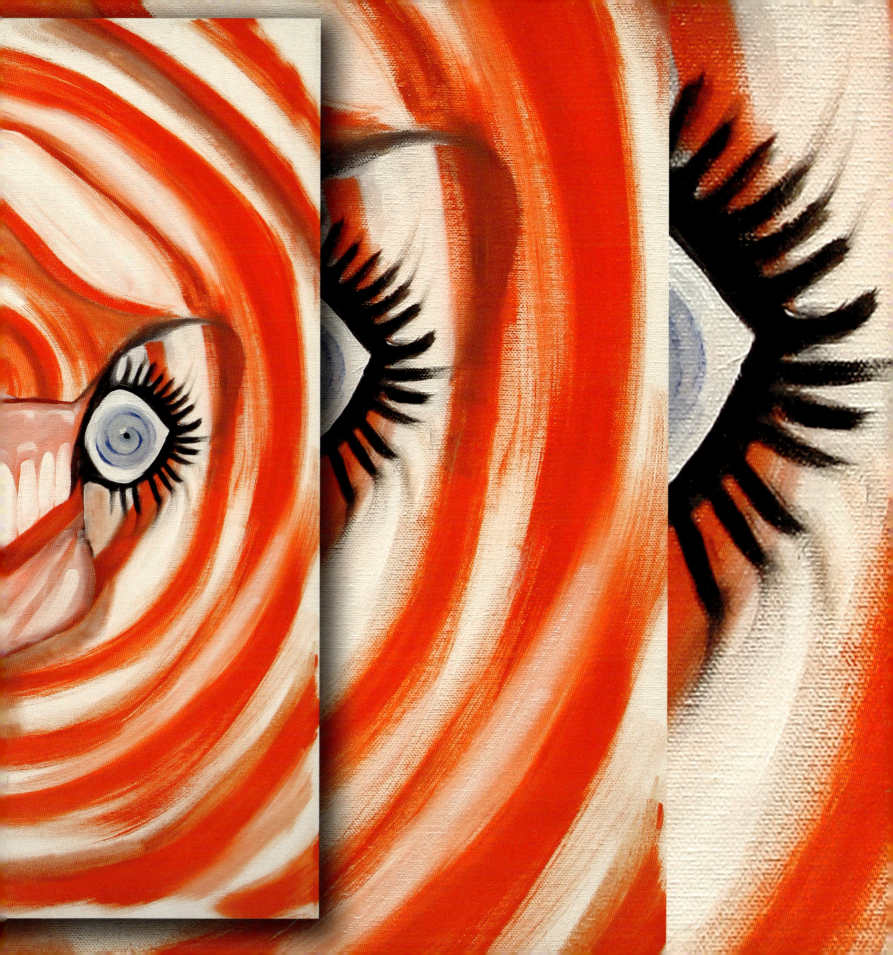

Think of a young, nerdy sort of child trying to get used to the cold water as he wades into a swimming pool: shivering, arms wrapped around himself, weak beady blue eyes looking naked without his glasses. "Physical activity must not be my thing," he tells himself, and no one makes an attempt to convince him otherwise. So the boy spends a lot of time indoors. He learns to draw, and we shouldn't be surprised that when he enters the grownup world, where money is at stake and where ego is at stake, he plays it safe and stays away from the big splashes. I think a lot of good artists start out like this little boy. Then there's the other kid—the one who draws because he embraces each opportunity that presents itself. He discovers what unique pleasures drawing and painting and creating are. It is my educated guess that Nate was that kid in the pool making big annoying splashes while kids like me were building up the courage to take off our shirts.

aaron philby

SNUB

The Bar

Drawing for tips at a bar, me and my buddy Eggz were just having a good ol' time as usual. He went off to draw some people at one table and I found this guy who looked like a drunken walrus at another. He had a **HUGE** gap and two big teeth that I just couldn't wait to exaggerate. I asked this guy if it was cool to draw him. He said "yeah sure," and passed me ten dollars.

I took my time so I could do a cool sketch. Right before I finished, a couple of rednecks came over and started to praise my drawing. I ripped it off and showed Walrus the finished piece. With a disgusted, pissed off, teary eyed look, Walrus asked for his money back. As I started to give it back, the smaller redneck got between us and said in a loud drunken voice, "This is an awesome drawing motherfucker! Pay up!"

Walrus just looked at me like he wanted to kill me, or at least sink his giant tusks into my head. The bigger redneck yelled at Walrus to leave as I sat there and said nothing. Then Walrus got up and started to come at me. Without hesitation, Big Redneck pushed Walrus all the way to the front door. Together The Rednecks shoved him out of the bar.

They were ranting about wanting to fight as they returned. Both said I did a great job. I was still just a rookie, so it was cool to see guys like that stand up for my art. But even though they were like a couple of heroes, I didn't want Walrus to get his ass whooped over a drawing.

Eggz came over to see what the fuss was all about. Big Redneck retold the story, and then asked Eggz to draw him. We all drank and bullshited about Walrus while Eggz sketched. The drawing was coming out pretty funny, which made Small Redneck's teeth wiggle out. Eggz ripped off the sketch to show the Big Redneck, who laughed out loud. Big Redneck then took the drawing, threw it on the floor, poured his beer all over it, and jumped up and down on it like a big baby.

After the tantrum, Big Redneck glared at Eggz like the Hulk preparing to smash up the bar. The small redneck quickly tried to restrain his drunken friend, which only created conflict between them. With content smiles, me and Eggz calmly stepped out of the bar unscathed.

Just another day on the job.

Stories

Events are always fun as a caricature artist. You dress up, bring your supplies, and draw as fun and crazy as you like. Well, at least I do. I love making crowds laugh, sometimes even more than making big tips.

One time, I was at a huge event with many other fellow artists. We all got separated throughout the party and I got to draw with one other awesome caricaturist. The night started out great as two ladies, fat and skinny, sat down to be drawn together. They wanted two separate drawings, one by each of us.

I started by drawing the nose of the fat lady. Right away I heard an, "Oink oink," from behind me. It was their friend making fun of how I drew the fat one's nose. Then Oinker wanted to get drawn into our sketches as well. These ladies had great energy, so I thought it would be a funny joke to draw her with hooves because she kept snorting and making fun of her friend. When we finished, we showed them our drawings. They laughed so hard as they walked off, and left us feeling like we did a nice job.

Three minutes later, two women came over to tell us that we couldn't draw funny anymore. Apparently, both of us had upset the ladies we just drew. In disbelief, we learned that Oinker was running the show. We were shocked, but I wasn't really worried because I knew they had a fun time and a good laugh.

Both me and the other guy were fired that day. Not sure who got the last laugh on this one.

Comic-Con '07

Comic-Con San Diego is the biggest pop culture and comic book convention in the world.

I was invited to do live caricatures at a booth to help promote the book "Rejects". Joining me that day was the infamous Gabe Hunt, a guy who could sell fire to ice and salt to a slug. We both tried to get people to sit down for a sketch, and it didn't take long before Gabe found a couple to sit for me.

The guy looked like Adrien Brody and his girlfriend looked like she was made of silicone. The couple had a weird presence about them. They loved to people watch, and as you may know, Comic-Con is awesome for that activity. But, under their breath, they were calling people ugly and stupid looking for dressing up like Jedi and Ghostbusters.

As I got closer to finishing the caricature, I had attracted a large group of people around me. The crowd started to laugh, and "Silicone" started looking worried. When I completed the drawing, I took a picture with my digital camera. Everyone was laughing pretty hard while I tore the drawing off my sketch pad and presented it to the couple.

Their faces turned completely blank as I handed it over to them. The boyfriend slowly took the sketch and they both looked at it in shock. Then Silicone quickly snatched the drawing from him and gently ripped it into as many pieces as she possibly could. Because of that, the crowd burst into thunderous laughter, and I couldn't help but to get up and laugh with them. There was only one way out of the booth and I was standing right there as Silicone got up and walked towards me. I looked directly into her eyes and said, "Thanks for sittin'."

She flipped me off and said, "Fuck you, asshole!" as she stormed away, leaving her man behind. He then apologized and offered me three bucks, promising that he would tape the pieces together at home. With a smile I told him, "Keep the money, your girlfriend just made my day."

That was the only reject at the booth.

People ask me, "How do you create such an extreme likeness?"

At times, some don't understand what they are looking at, or can't understand what a unique likeness is when arranged in an abstract or extreme way.

Our perspectives are infinite. This is why there are so many original styles with unique views of the same subjects. This also may explain why there might be disagreements on the rendered likeness of a person.

You can learn methods and perfect your technique. You can learn my process and try to understand my theory. You can strive all you want to see things the way I do or try and make other people see eye to eye with you, but our perspectives will never be exactly the same.

That is the beauty of the human connection and why we are all so interesting and unique.

THIN

Taking **EXAGGERATION** to **higher levels** can of course be very complex. Then when you get to that point where your **eyeballs** bungee out of your **SKULL** and dance in your lap watching the world fold into inside out protons and long johns, when the likeness is so ABSTRACT that it can be hard to keep up with anything further, then it becomes like trying to make sure no dishes break during an **earthquake**.

Color can be pushed with a technique I like to call color DRAINING. Take a color and **intensify** it by >concentrating< it into one area. Once that has gone beyond> the limits, sound of the subject can get **louder** by exaggerating WAY THE SUBJECT LOOKS AND ACTS.

KING KAP

A face and body is the **STRUCTURE** of which defines a recognizable look, UNIQUELY different from any other, but with the same necessary features. Color of the face and body defines a unique reflection of light. Sound is a unique vibration of facial and body language. All put together causes unique **attractions**, reflections, and **reactions**. This is essence.

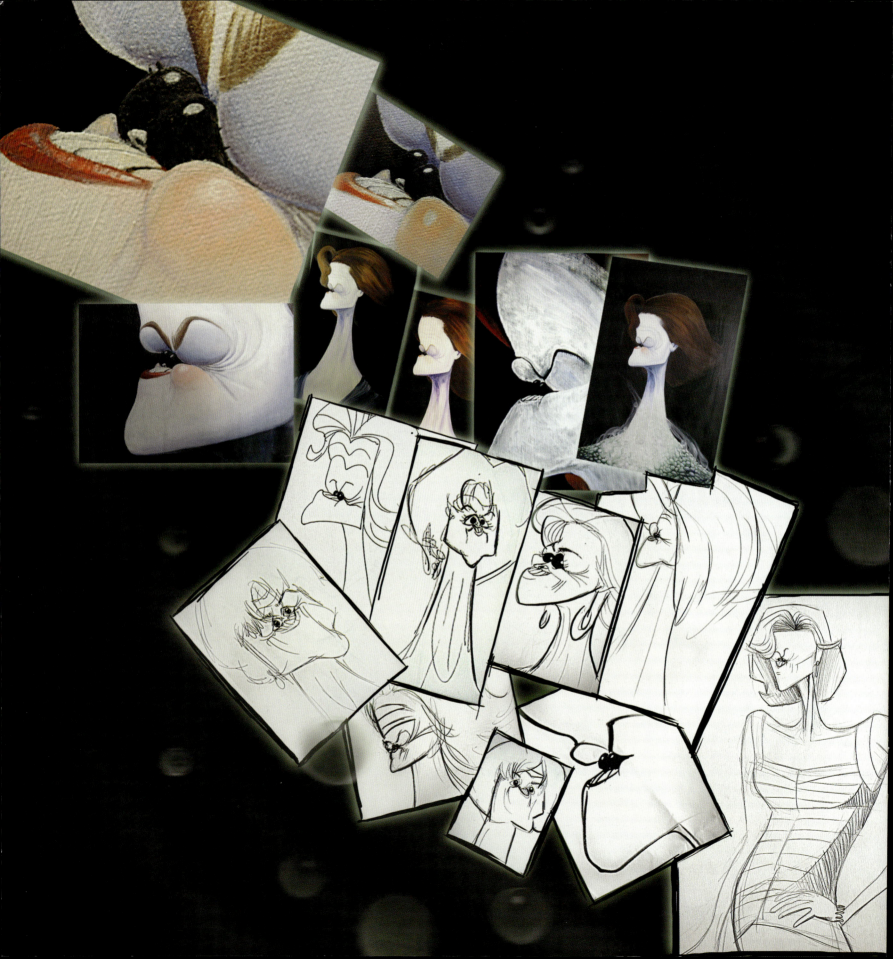

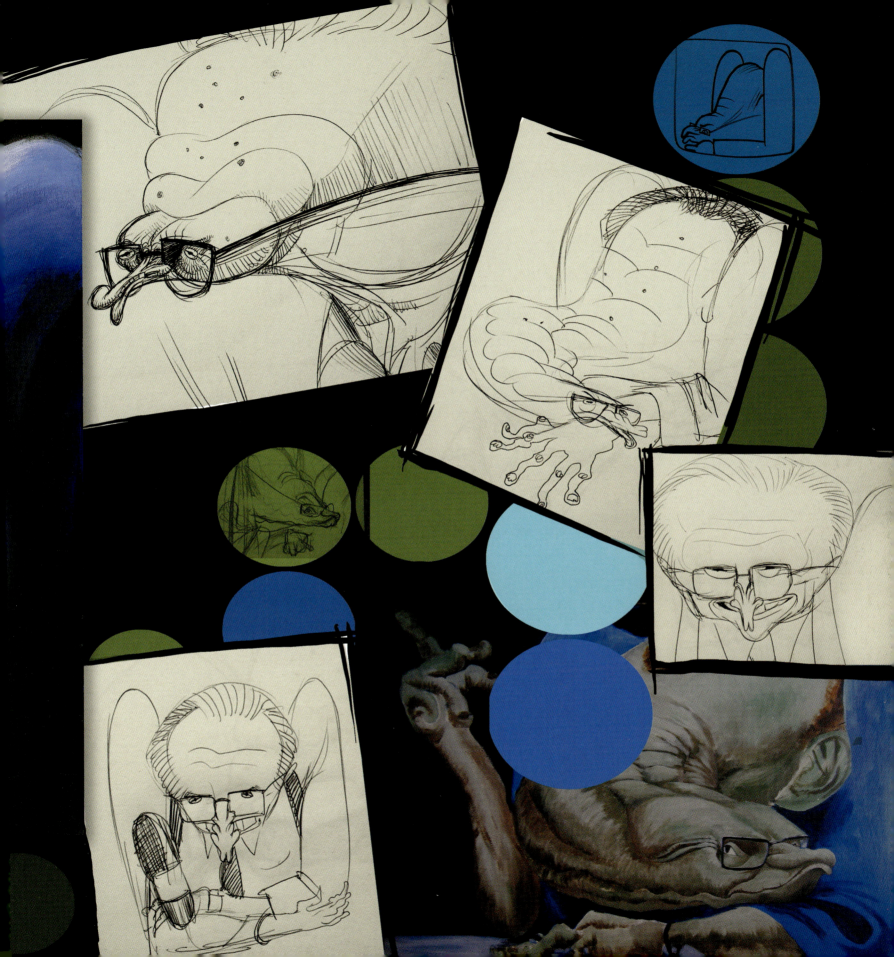

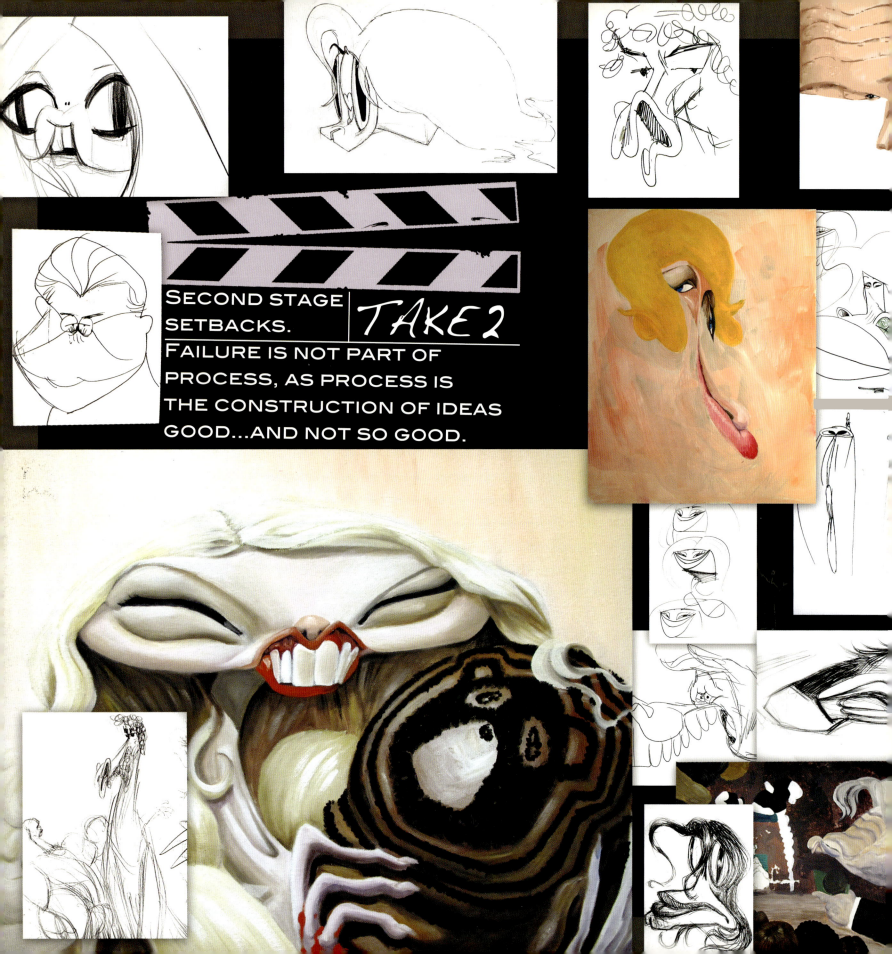

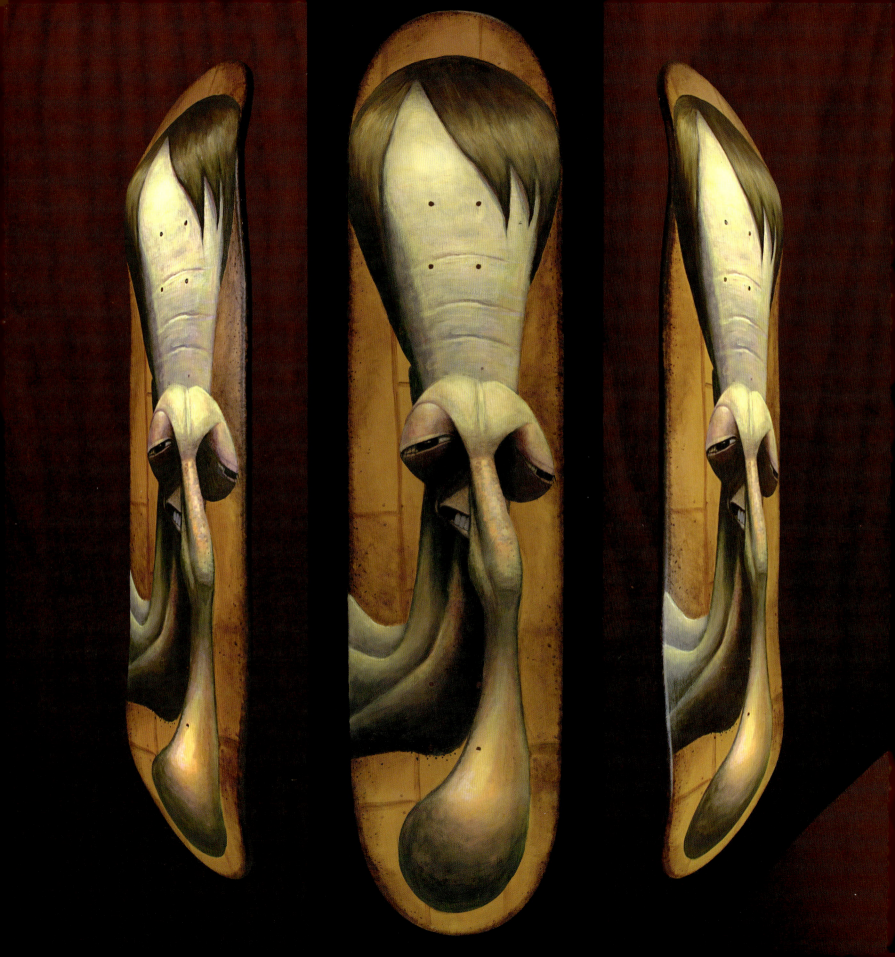

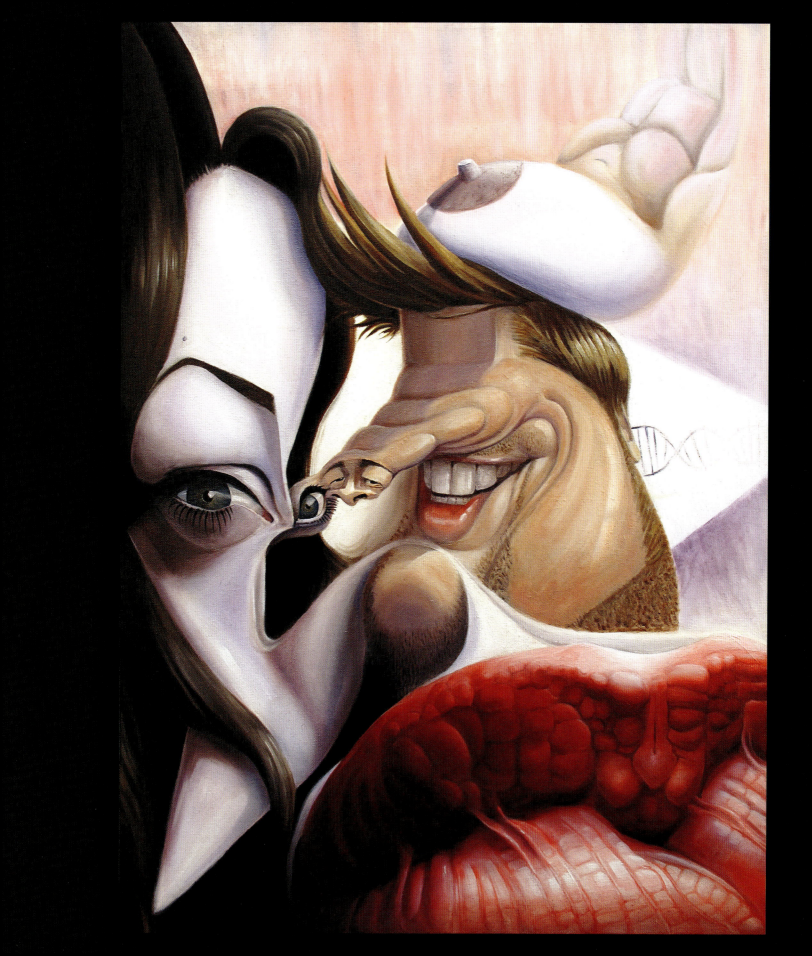

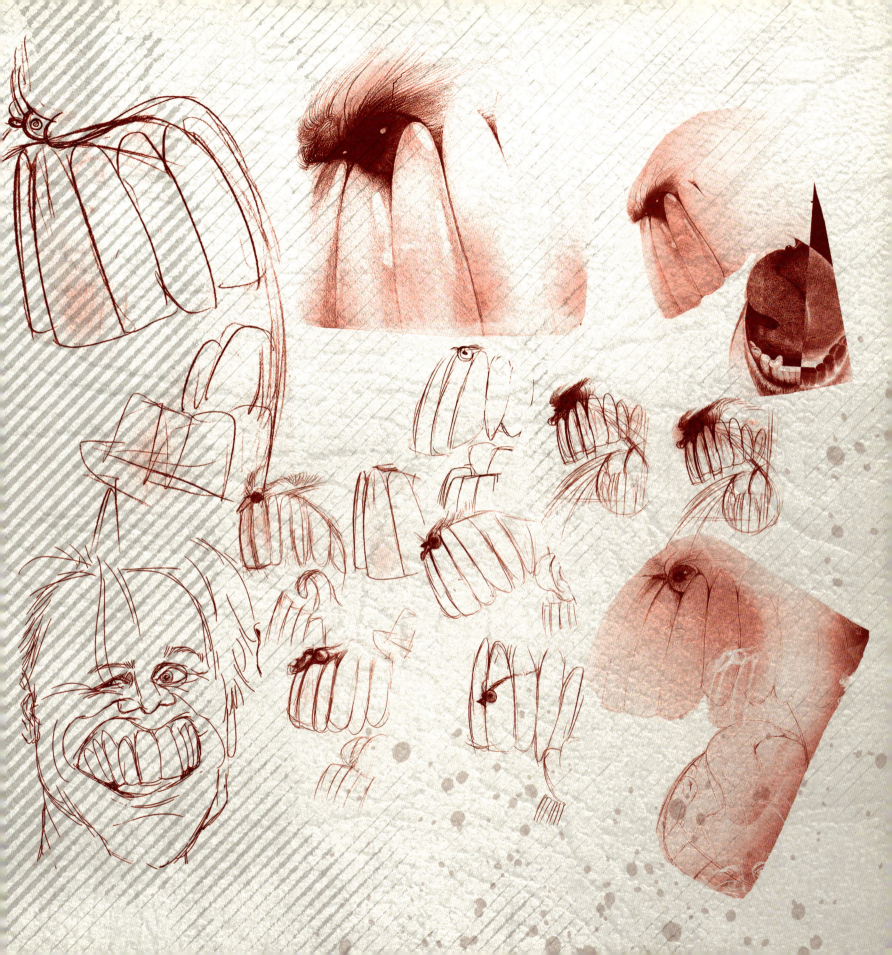

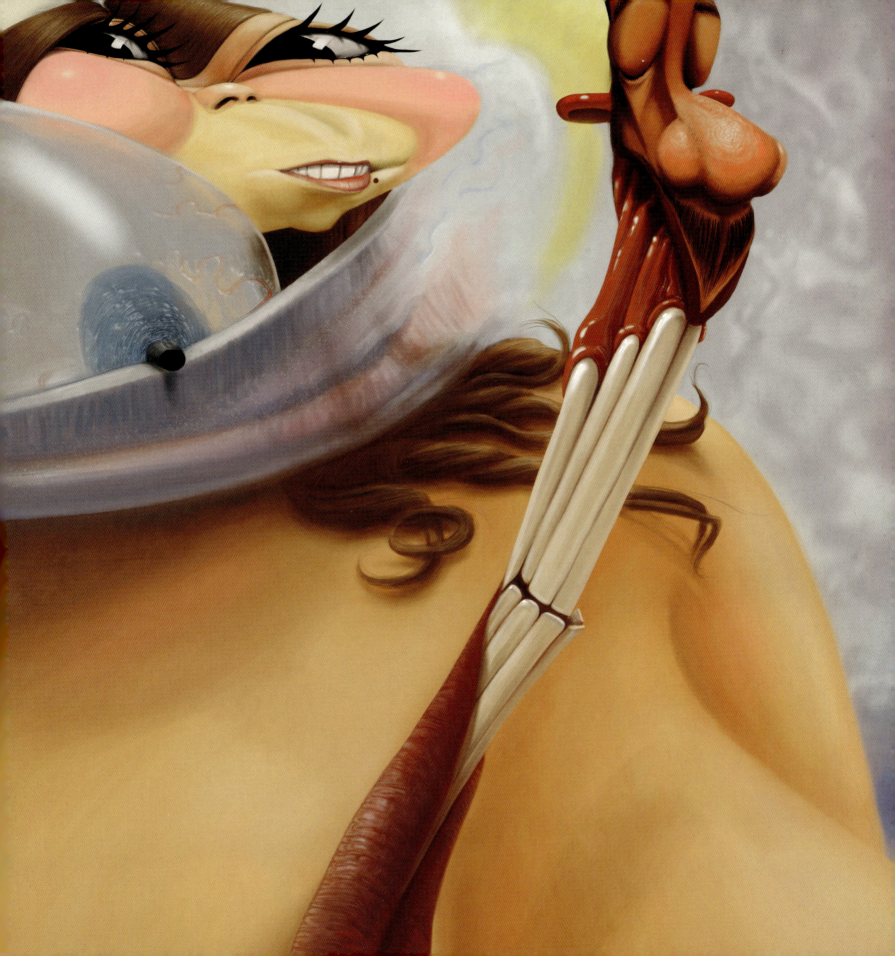

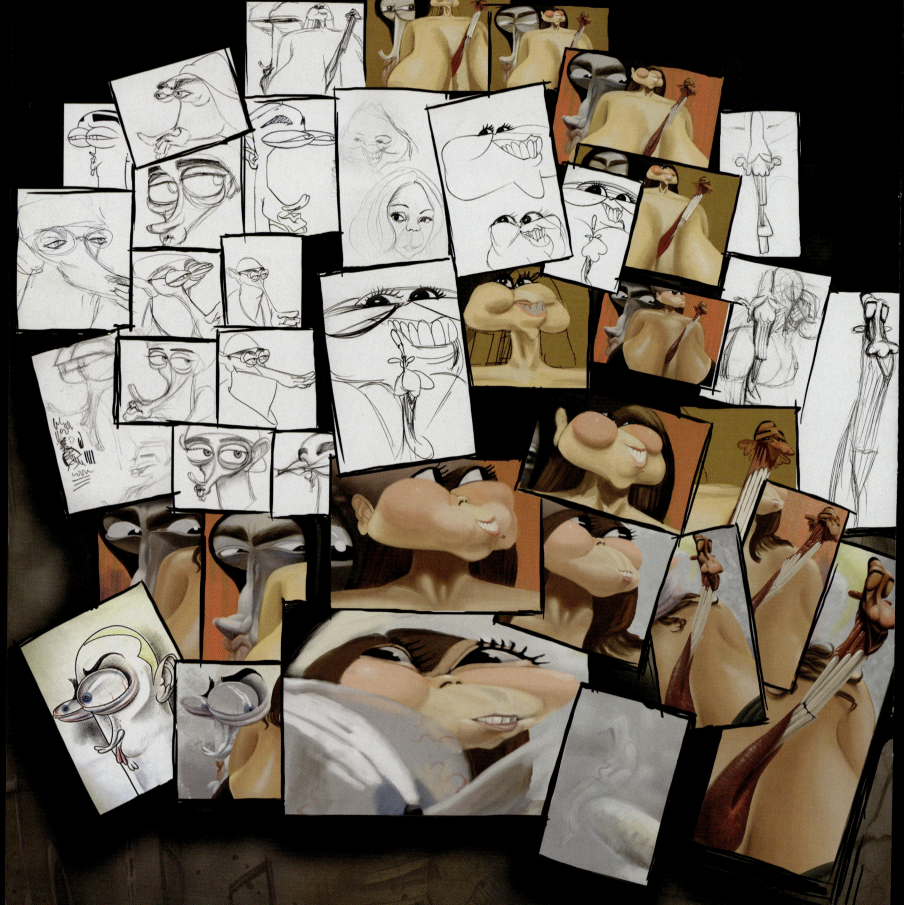

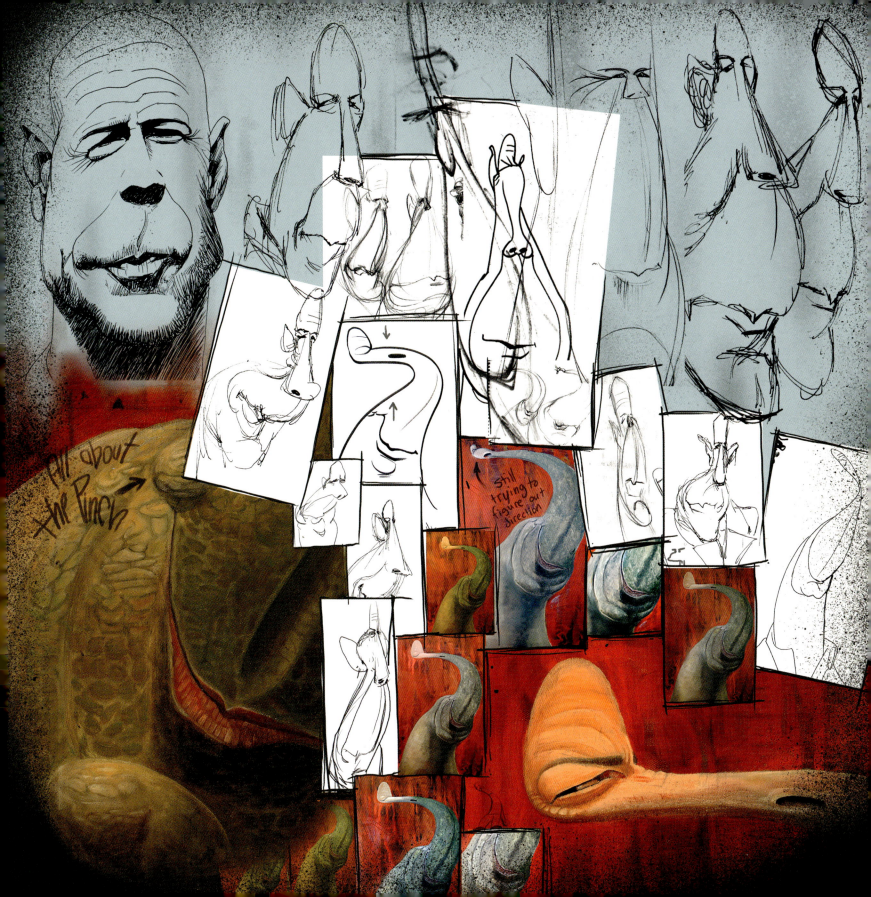

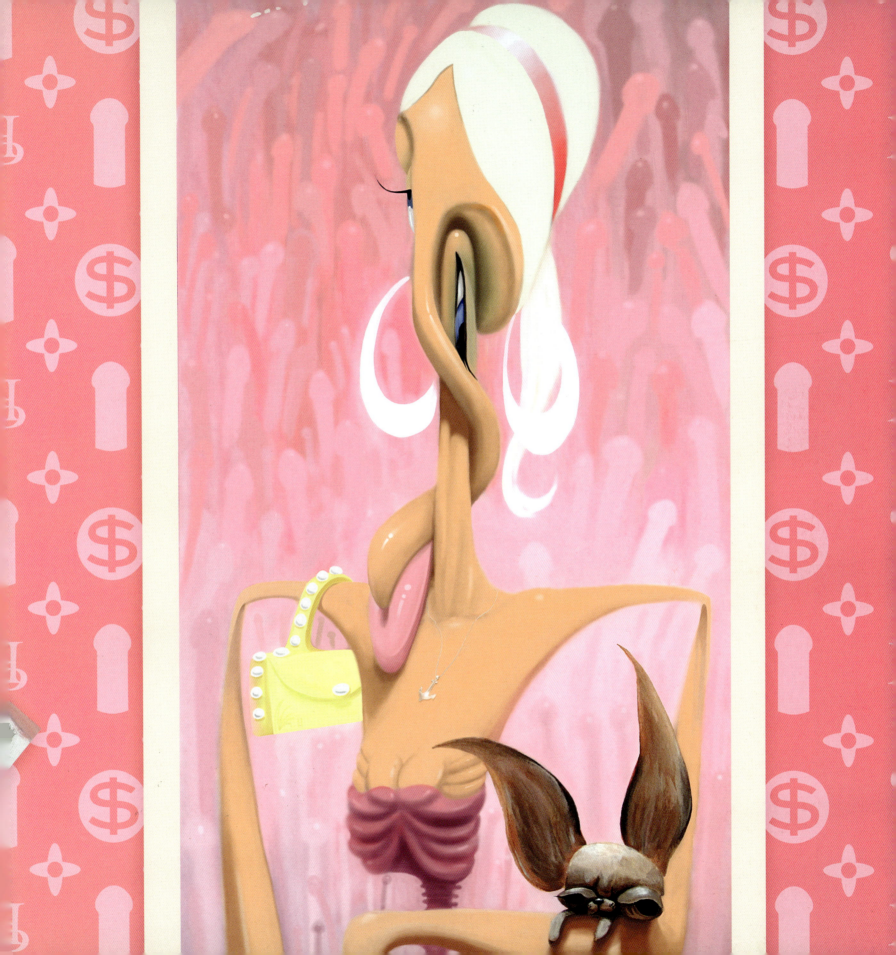

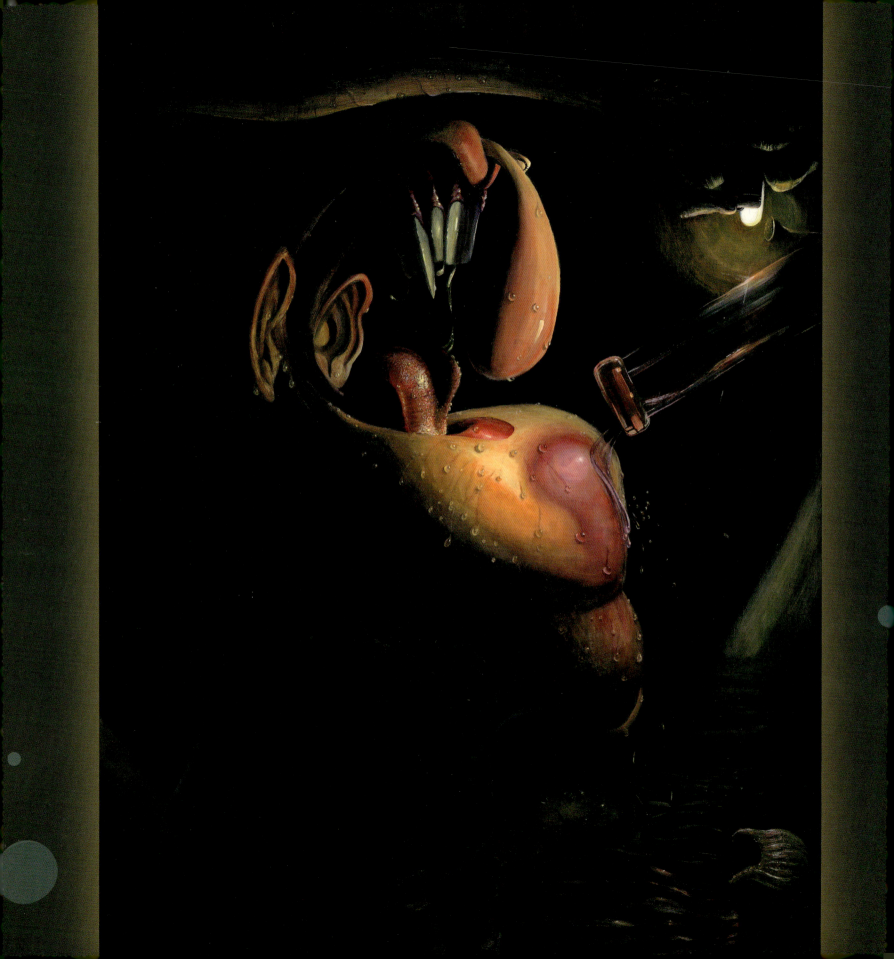

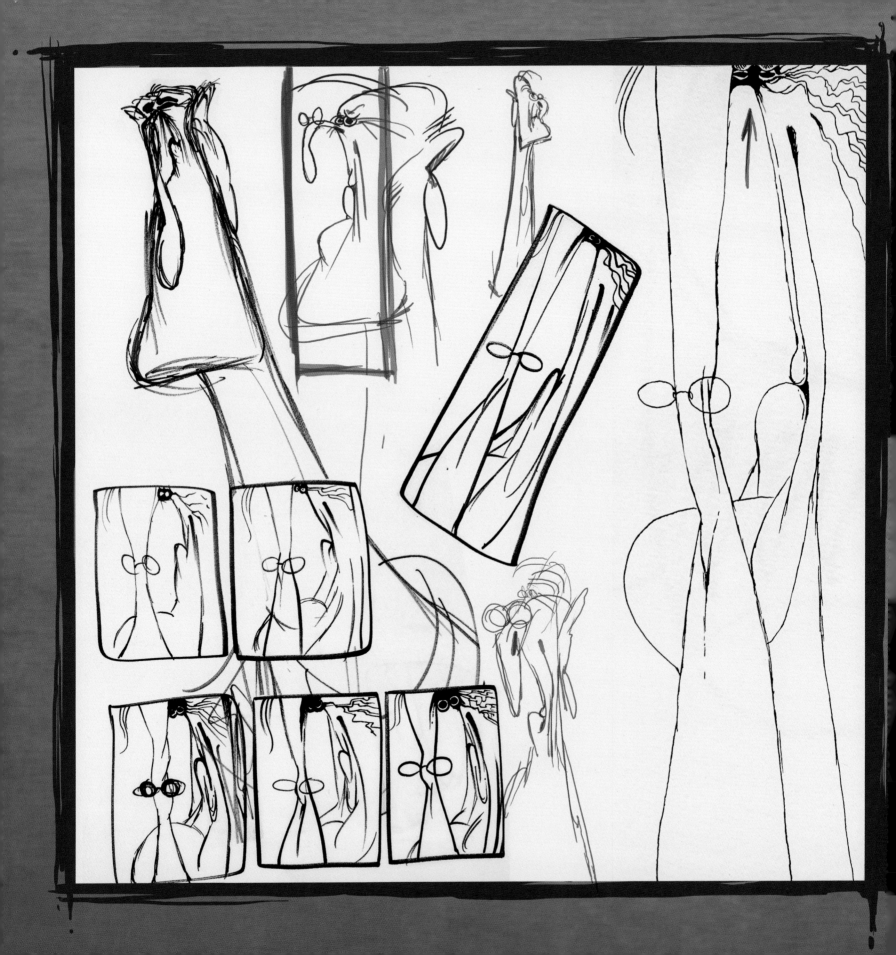

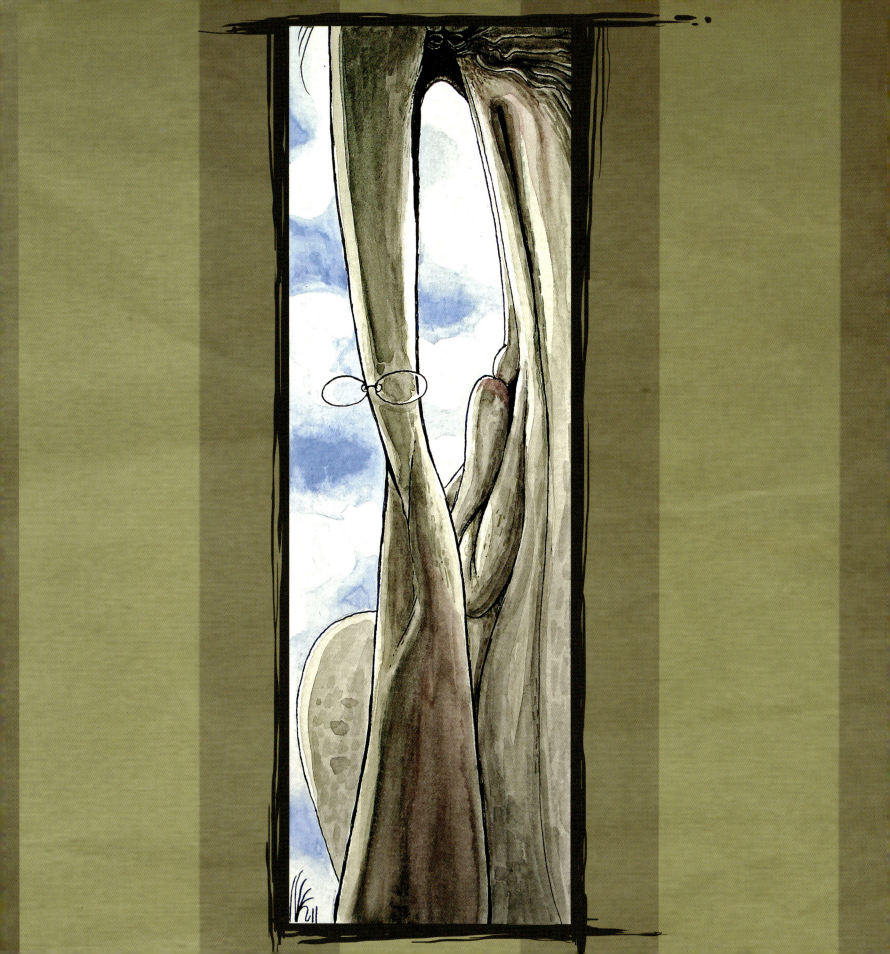

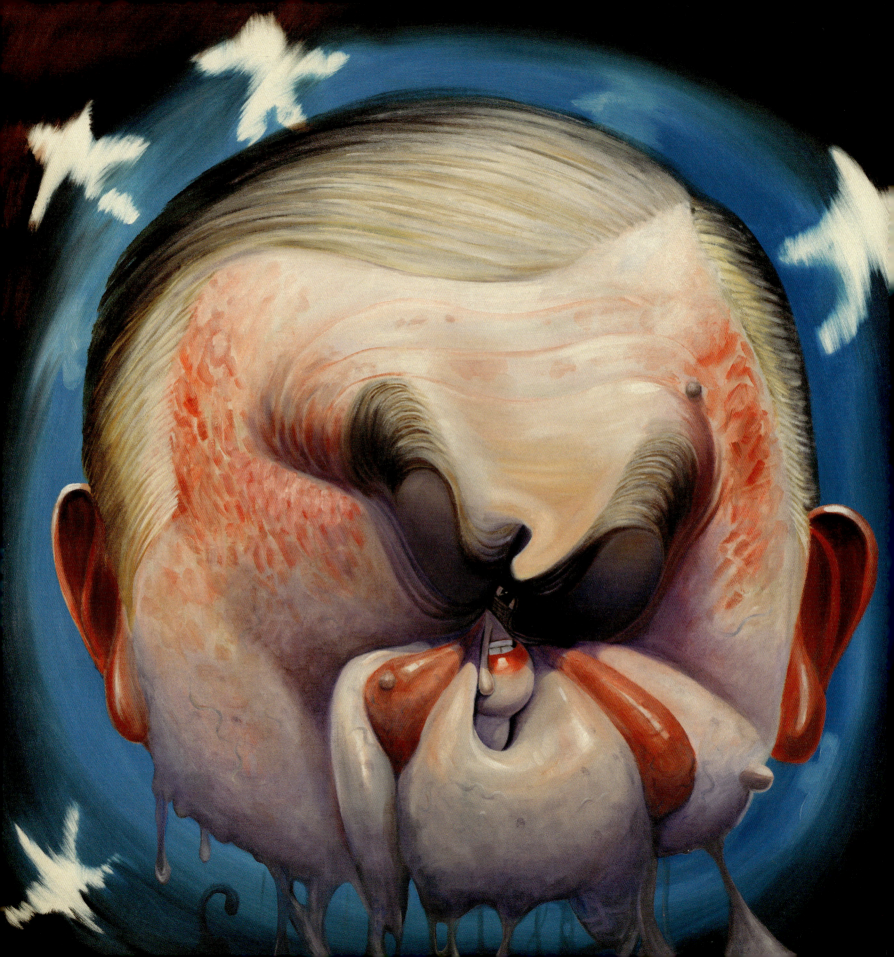

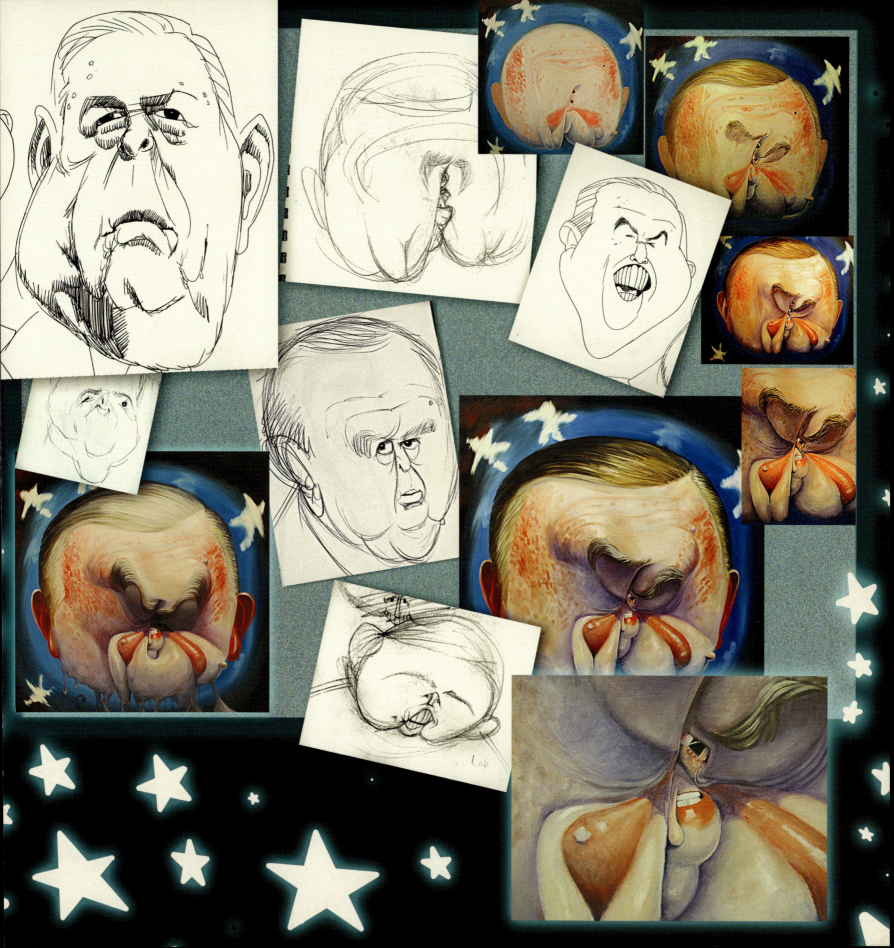

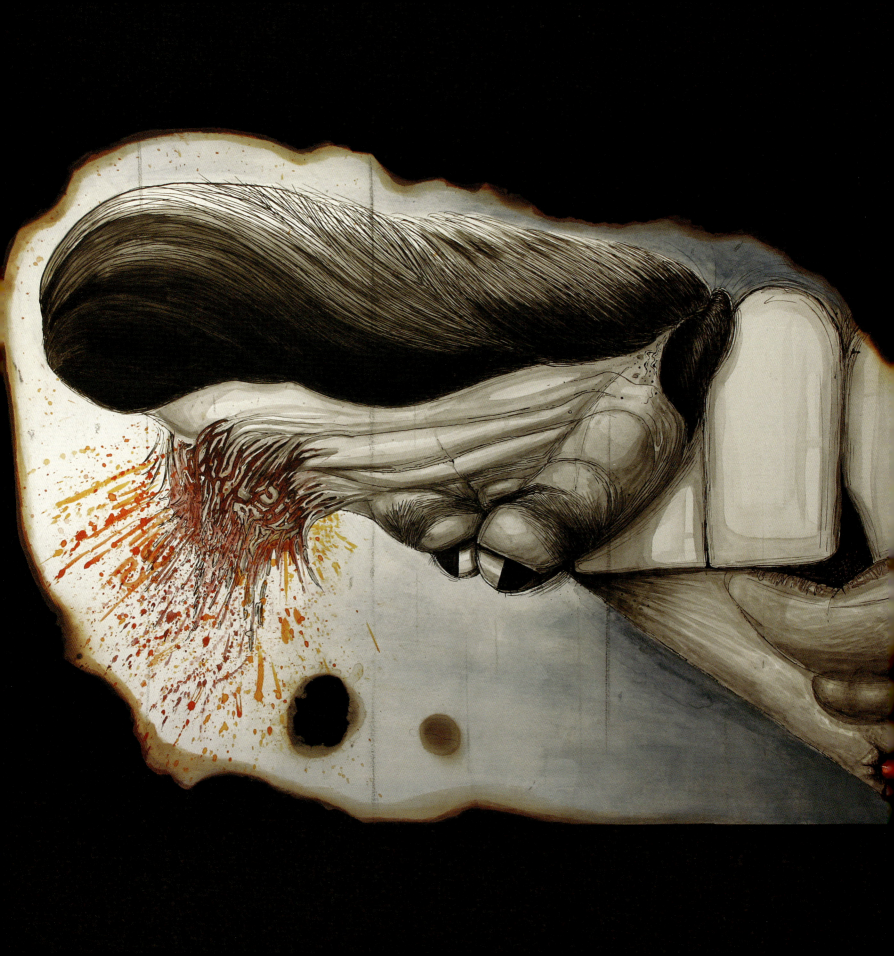

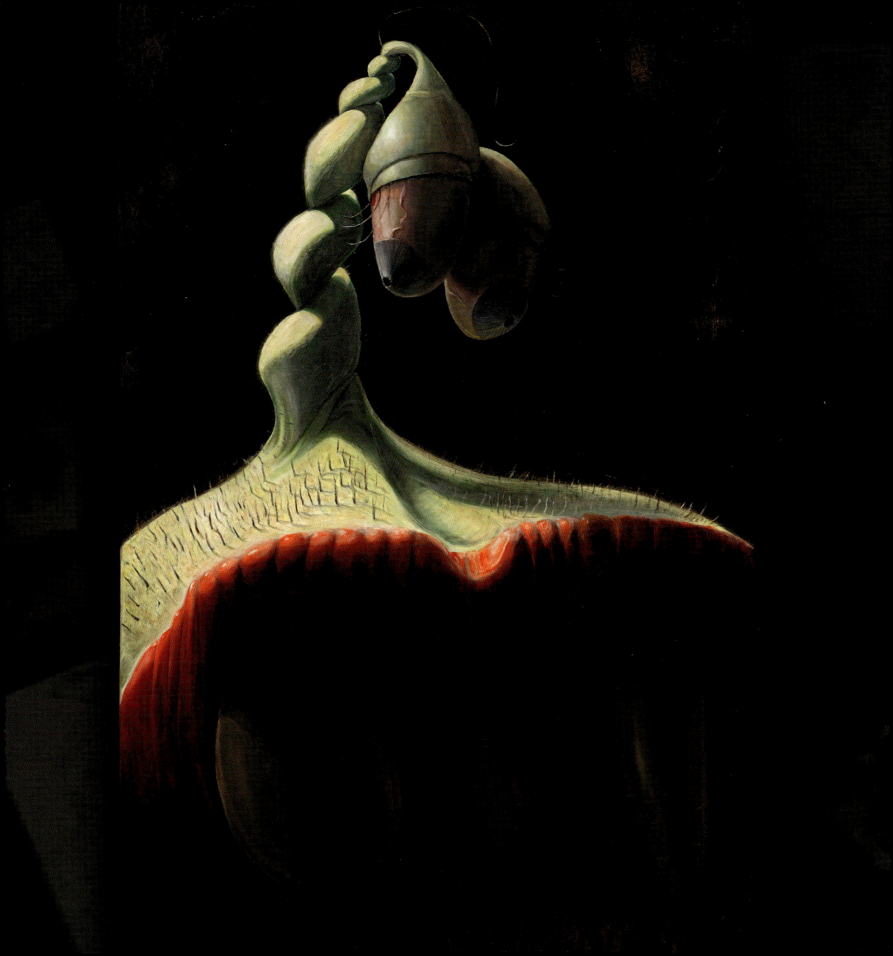

I do not paint a portrait to look like a subject, rather does the person grow to look like his portrait.

Salvador Dali

Table of FACES

Coach Phil
acrylic

Kyle Mc
digital

Julia Roberts
oil

Bruce Bruce
oil

ConAndy
acrylic

Britney Spears
digital

Stanley Baker
acrylic

Seth Rogen
acrylic

Bird
digital

Harland
marker

Tom Hanks
acrylic

Cosby
acrylic
oil

Take 1
Quarter

Michael Cera
digital

Julia Stiles
acrylic

Tommy Jones
pen/ink
watercolor

George Jr
acrylic

Jason Lee
acrylic

Frank Miller
oil

Katie Couric
oil

Penelope
acrylic
digital

Sean Penn
acrylic

Queen Liz 3
oil
acrylic

23 Ellen
oil

24 Steve Carell
pen/ink
watercolor

25 Sigourney
oil

26 Leguizamo
digital

27 Letterman
acrylic

28 James Cromwell
pen/ink
watercolor

29 Missy
digital

30 Larry King
acrylic

HALFTIME

Middle Word

Snubs

Thinking Kap

32
House Laurie
acrylic

31
Snoop
acrylic

36
Tony Hawk
acrylic

37
Brangelina
oil

34
Liv
digital

33
Julia
oil

38
Bob
ink/marker
artstick

39
David Lynch
oil
digital

Take 2
Quarter

35
Obama
pencil
watercolor

40
Gary Busey
pencil
watercolor

41
MariEm Cannon
digital

42
Bruce Willis
oil

43
Dr Death
acrylic

44
Paris
acrylic
digital

45
Phelps
acrylic

46
James Cromwell
pen/ink
watercolor

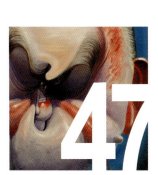

47
Lou Dobbs
oil

48
Nicole Kidman
oil

49
JFK
pen/ink
watercolor

50
Buscemi
oil

For more info on each piece please visit natekapnicky.com

SPECIAL THANKS

Dez.Goodwin.Philby
Diego.Beau.Silver
Moyse.Jared.Urzua
Oakes.Sakoda.James
Devon. Chrome Digital
Tiffany.Mom.Dad.Doug
All the famous people
for being famous

My X-box for breaking

BEASTED

Copyright © 2012 Nate Kapnicky

All artwork presented in this book is copyright © 2012 Nate Kapnicky.

Any similarity, without satiric purpose, to any person, living or dead, portrayed or depicted in this book is purely coincidental.

All rights reserved. No part of this book may be reproduced or used in any format or in any medium without the written permission of the publisher.

Published by

Kap Art
San Diego, CA
kapart@nathankapnicky.com

Printed in China

ISBN-13: 978-0-9854748-0-5

First printing, 2012

Natekapnicky.com

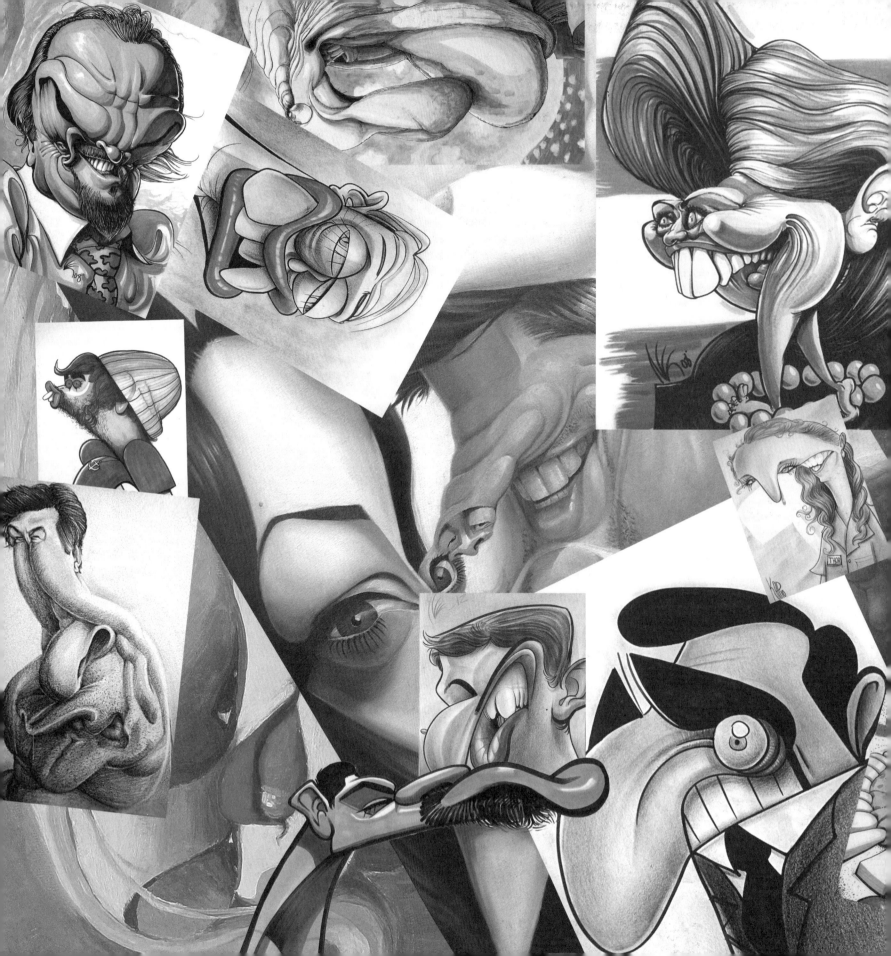